Library of Congress Cataloging-in-Publication Data:

Names: Eggers, Dave, author. | Harris, Shawn (Artist), illustrator.
Title: Her right foot / story by Dave Eggers ; art by Shawn Harris.
Description: San Francisco, California : Chronicle Books, 2017. |
Audience: Ages 5-8. | Audience: K to Grade 3. Identifiers: LCCN 2016057953
| ISBN 9781452162812 (alk. paper) Subjects: LCSH: Monuments—United
States—Juvenile literature. | Historic sites—United States—Juvenile literature.
Classification: LCC E159 .E39 2017 | DDC 973—dc23 LC record available at
https://lccn.loc.gov/2016057953

Manufactured in United States of America.

Design by Shawn Harris and Kristine Brogno.
Typeset in Acta.
The illustrations in this book were rendered
in construction paper and India ink.

10 9 8 7 6 5 4 3 2 1

Chronicle Books LLC
680 Second Street
San Francisco, California 94107

Chronicle Books—we see things differently.
Become part of our community at www.chroniclekids.com.

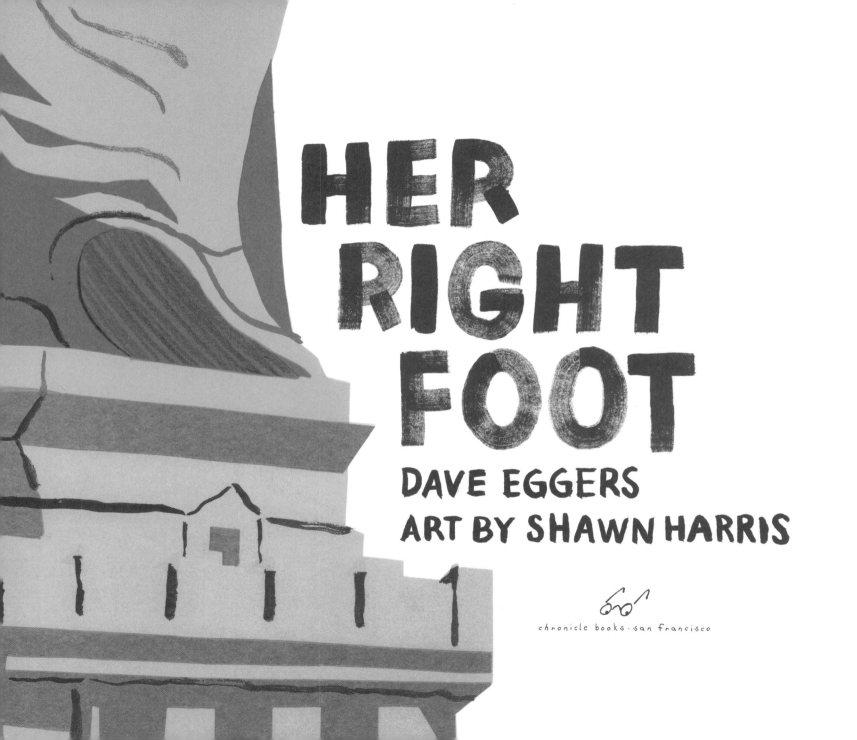

HER RIGHT FOOT

DAVE EGGERS

ART BY SHAWN HARRIS

chronicle books · san francisco

You have likely heard of a place called France.

If you have heard of France, you may have heard of the French.
They are the people who live in France.

You may have also heard of something called the Statue of Liberty.

Did you know that the
Statue of Liberty comes from France?

This is true. This is a factual book.

One day a Frenchman named Édouard de Laboulaye had an idea. The idea was to celebrate the 100 years the United States of America had been around by giving them a giant sculpture.

So he convinced another Frenchman, a Frenchman with an Italian last name, to design the sculpture. This artist's name was Frédéric Auguste Bartholdi. Bartholdi designed the statue.

He first made very small models of the sculpture, then larger ones, and finally one that is the one we know, which stands 305 feet above the water.

This final, full-size version was covered with a thin copper skin. The skin is about as thick as two pennies. That is not very thick!

TWO PENNIES

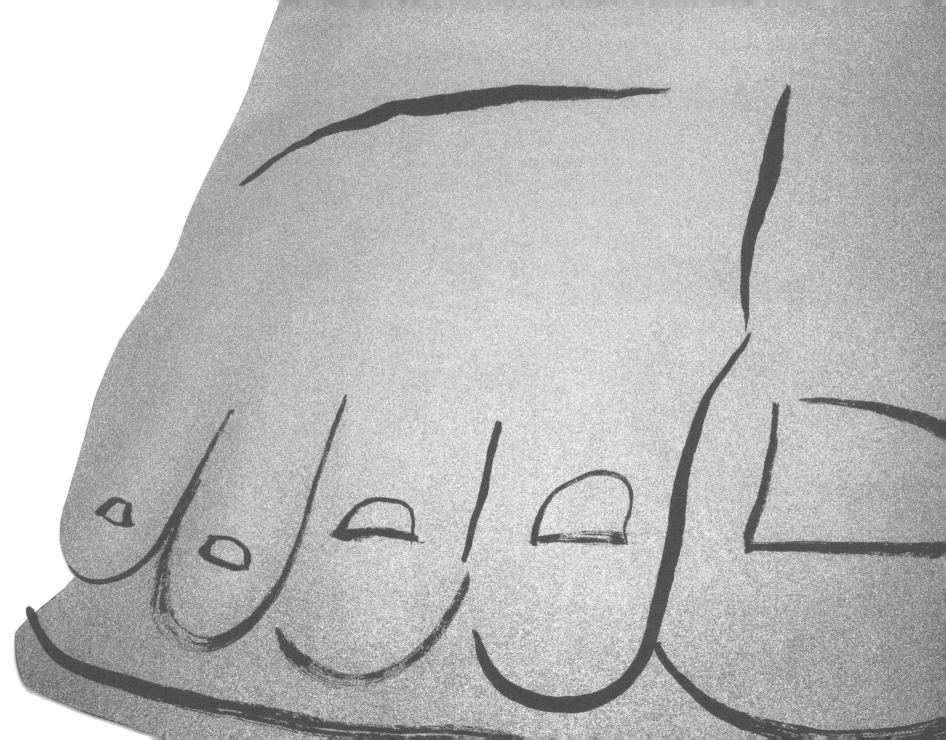

Here is a rendering of Bartholdi and his team—he had a team; he did not work alone; he did not like working alone—constructing the statue's hand.

Notice that the hand is bigger than these men. Thus they made the statue in many parts.

These parts were assembled in New York City.

No, wait. First they were assembled in Paris. Did you know this? Ask your friends and even your teachers if they knew that before the Statue of Liberty was assembled in New York, she was first constructed in Paris. Your friends and teachers will be astounded. They will be impressed. They might think you are fibbing.

But you are not fibbing. This really happened. The Statue of Liberty stood there, high above Paris, for almost a year, in 1884.

After they assembled the statue in Paris, they took it apart.

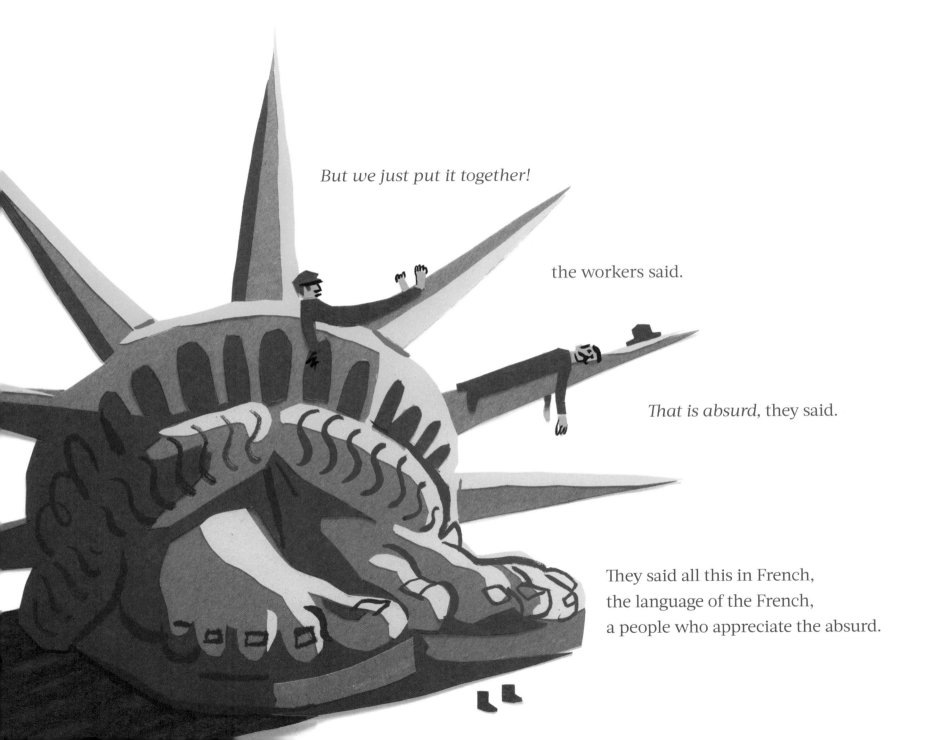

But we just put it together!

the workers said.

That is absurd, they said.

They said all this in French,
the language of the French,
a people who appreciate the absurd.

In 1885, after they took it apart, they put the parts in 214 crates, and put these crates on a boat. The boat was called the *Isère*. The boat traveled over the Atlantic Ocean and made its way to a city called New York, which is in a state also called New York.

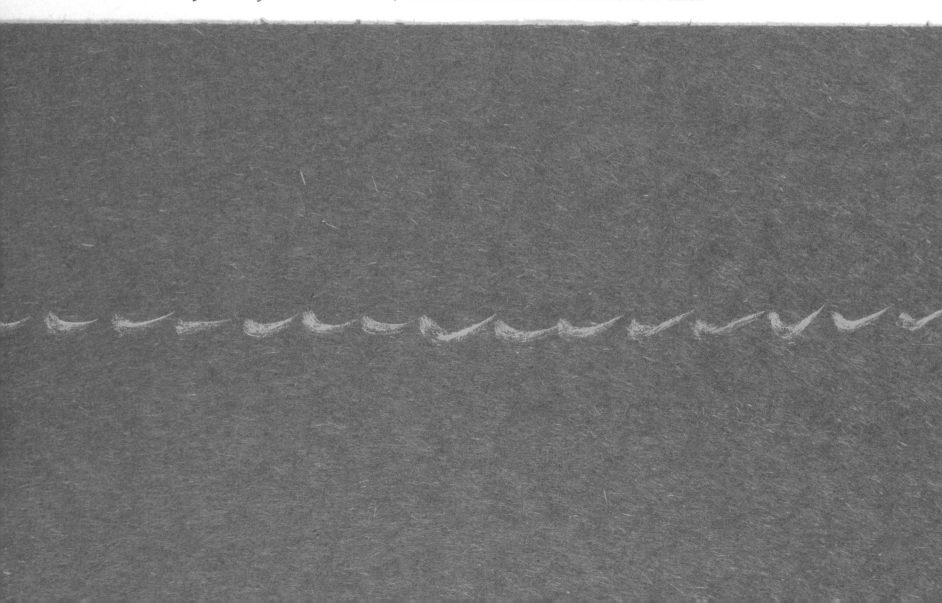

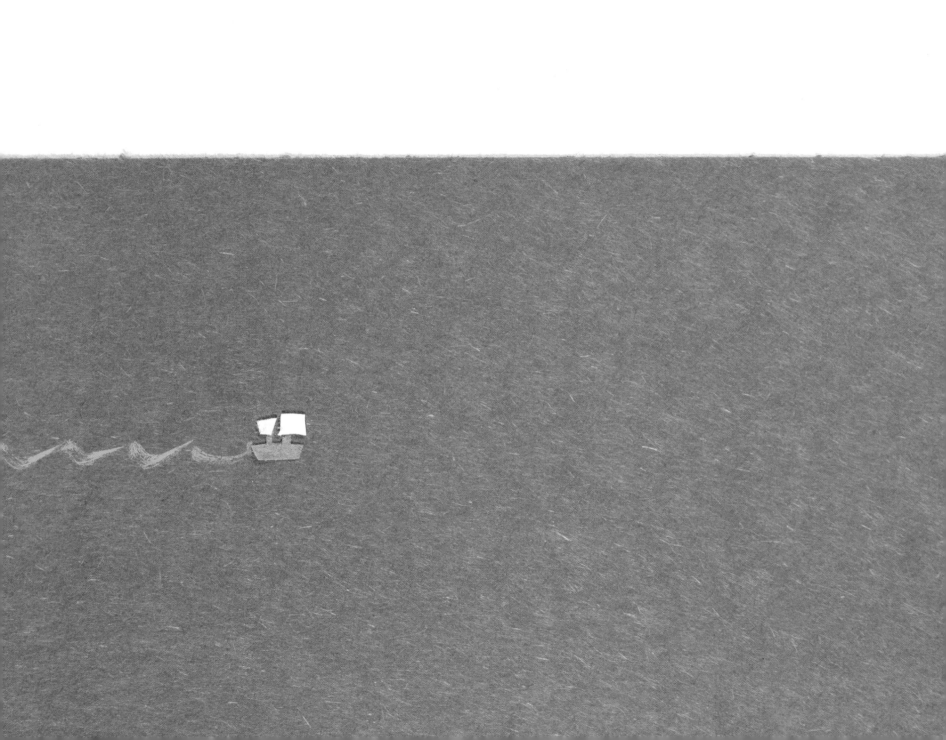

EAST RIVER

WILLIAMSBURG   BUSHWICK

B R

EAST
VILLAGE

LOWER EAST
SIDE

DUMBO

MANHATTAN

CHINATOWN

GREENWICH
VILLAGE

SOHO

TRIBECA

BATTERY
PARK

HUDSON RIVER

UPPER

NEW
JERSEY

ELLIS

ISLAND

PARK SLOPE

CONEY ISLAND

FLATBUSH

OOKLYN

BROOKLYN HEIGHTS

RED HOOK

SUNSET PARK

BAY RIDGE

THE ATLANTIC OCEAN

GOVERNOR'S ISLAND

N Y BAY

Hundreds of workers (perhaps 214 of them) took the pieces out of the 214 boxes, then began to rivet the pieces together. Assembling the statue took 17 months, and it all happened on what was then called Bedloe's Island.

BEDLOE'S ISLAND

Bartholdi liked to see the sculpture rise above the harbor. Sometimes he watched the construction from the water. Sometimes he watched it from the land. Usually he was wearing a sturdy black hat, for he, like most European men of the time, favored sturdy black hats.

You may have noticed by now that the pictures of the Statue of Liberty in this book have her colored brown. You may have thought the illustrator of this book was not so good at his job, because we all know the Statue of Liberty to be a certain greenish-blue. But the Statue of Liberty was made of copper, and copper starts out brown.

Then, very slowly, when left outside for long periods of time, copper will eventually oxidize, and when it does, it turns this blue-green color.

So the Statue of Liberty that everyone in New York saw being constructed was actually brown. The Statue of Liberty, in fact, was brown for about thirty-five years.

The statue turned green around 1920, and has been this color ever since.
Perhaps you already knew this.

And you may have known that the book the statue is carrying, the one in her left hand, features the date, July 4, 1776, on which the Declaration of Independence was signed.

And you may know that the seven spikes on her crown represent the seven seas on Earth, and the seven continents, and the sun's rays, too.

And you probably know that the torch she carries
is a symbol of enlightenment, lighting the path to
liberty and freedom.

And you might have known that at one point, Thomas Edison, inventor of the lightbulb and the record player, once proposed to have a giant record player inside the Statue of Liberty. He did! He wanted the statue to be able to speak. In the end, though, this idea was considered a bit strange and was not pursued.

And did you know that the interior of the statue was designed by another Frenchman by the name of Eiffel? That's right—the same Eiffel who, a few years later, would design the Eiffel Tower.

And did you know that while the statue was first being constructed in Paris, a bunch of Parisians, mostly writers—they like to eat— actually dined in the area just below the statue's knee?

This, too, is true. While the statue was rising, Bartholdi set up a lunch, four stories up, to impress and enthrall these French writers, who, being difficult to impress and enthrall, were at least mildly amused.

But there is one thing that you might not know, and this is the central point to this book—a point the author apologizes for taking so long to get to.

The point is that even if you have seen a picture of the Statue of Liberty, or many pictures of the Statue of Liberty, or even hundreds of pictures of the Statue of Liberty, you probably have not seen pictures of her feet.

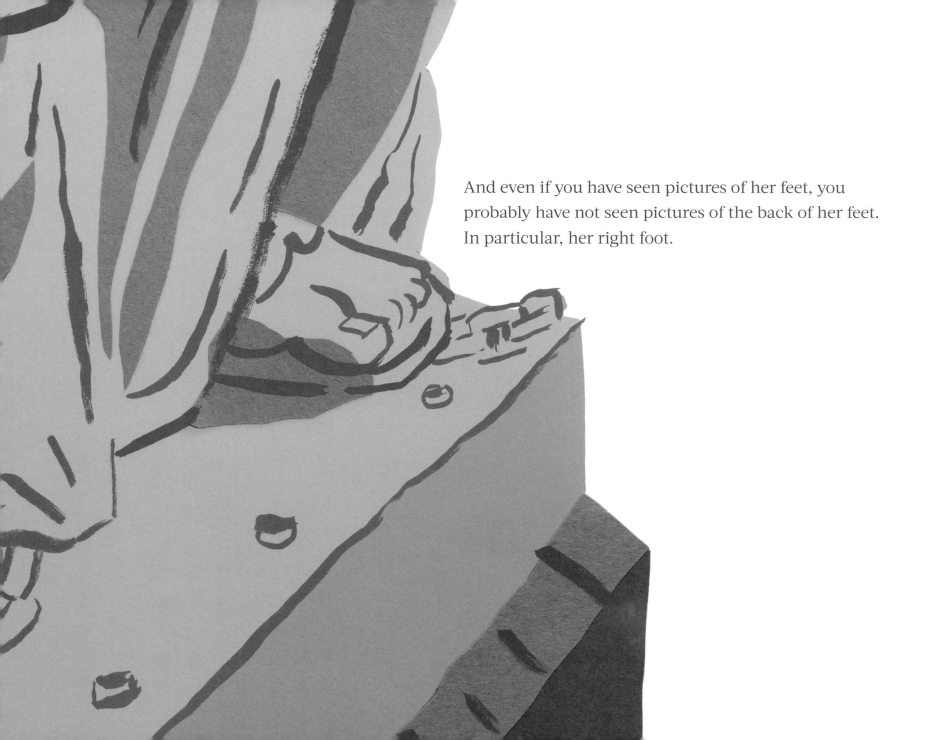

And even if you have seen pictures of her feet, you probably have not seen pictures of the back of her feet. In particular, her right foot.

What do you notice when you see this picture?

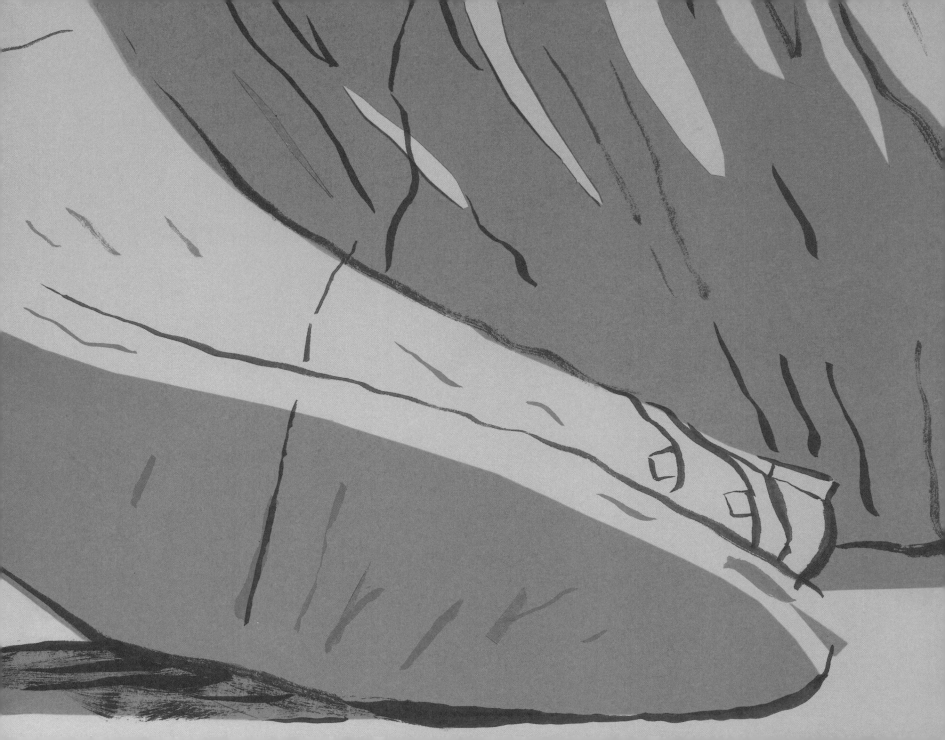

That's right! She is going somewhere! She is on the move!

Let's pause here and collect ourselves, and think about this.

Let's discuss this. Let's think about and discuss the fact that this is the largest sculpture in all the land, and the most iconic symbol of the United States of America. Let's talk about the fact that this statue has welcomed millions of visitors and immigrants to the USA.

People talk about her unusual headwear.

They talk about her gown, which seems a very heavy kind of garment, and would likely result in serious lower back issues.

They talk about her beautiful torch,

and the severe look on her face.

But no one talks about the fact that she is walking!
This 150-foot woman is on the go!

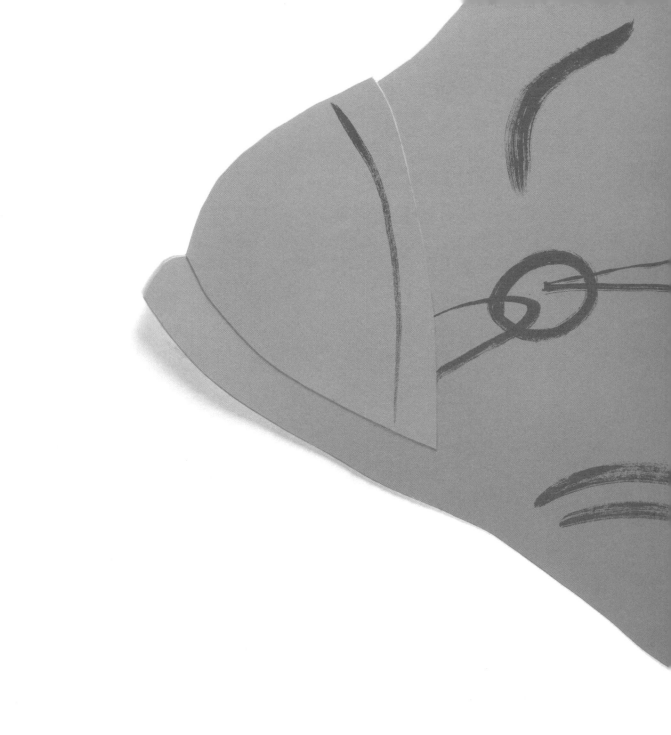

Every time we see the Statue of Liberty in pictures, or any time we imagine the Statue of Liberty, we see her standing still. Very still. Like, well, a statue.

But she is *moving.* She weighs 450,000 pounds and wears a size 879 shoe, and she is *moving.* How can we all have missed this? Or even if we saw this, and noticed this, how is it that we have seen and noticed a 450,000-pound human on her way somewhere and said, *Eh. Just another 150-foot woman walking off a 150-foot pedestal*?

And most important, where is she going?
Is she going to SoHo to get a panini?

Is she going to the West Village to look for vintage Nico records?

No, no. She is facing southwest, so she is facing New Jersey.
Could she be going to Trenton?

TRENTON MAKES THE WORLD TAKES

Wait. No. She is facing south*east*. So she is not going to New Jersey. But she is going somewhere. But where? Why is she moving?

There are certain things we know. We know that around her feet are chains. They are broken chains, implying that she has freed herself from bondage. We know that Bartholdi wanted us to know this. He wanted us to see the chains. People have talked about the chains.

But few talk about the foot that is so obviously in mid-stride. About the fact that her entire right *leg* is in mid-stride.

What does this mean? What does this mean that we often forget about this right foot, this right leg?

Here is an idea.

Here is a theory.

Here is a reminder.

If the Statue of Liberty is a symbol of freedom,
if the Statue of Liberty has welcomed millions
of immigrants to the United States, then how
can she stand still?

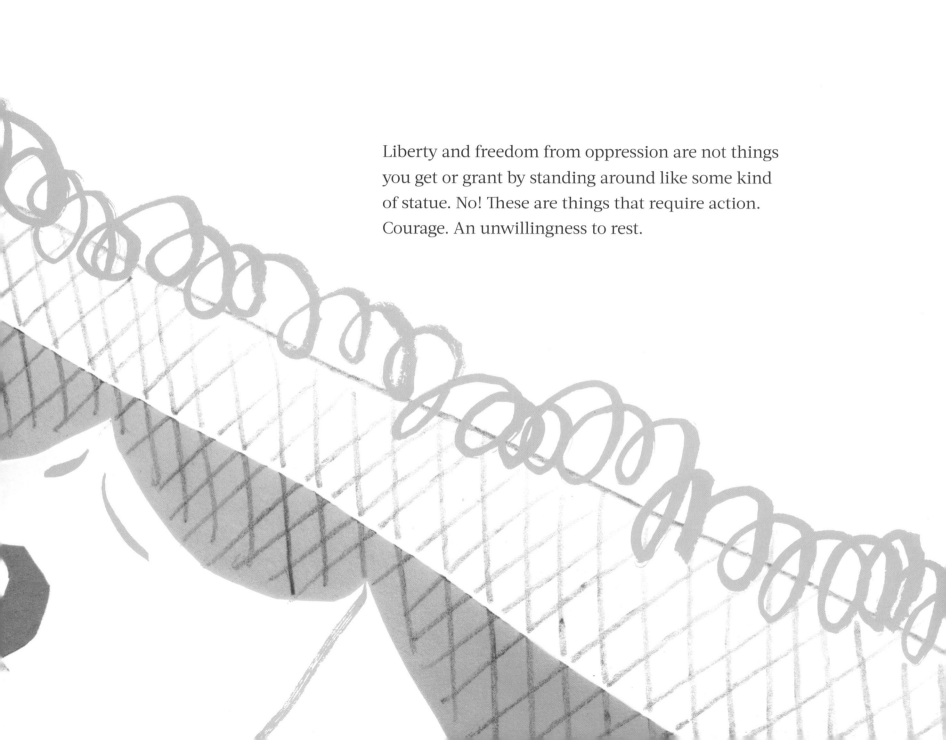

Liberty and freedom from oppression are not things you get or grant by standing around like some kind of statue. No! These are things that require action. Courage. An unwillingness to rest.

The Statue of Liberty was not built to welcome just 1,886 immigrants from Italy on one certain Sunday in, say, 1886.

No! She was built to welcome 3,000 immigrants from Poland the next day.

The next day, 5,000 Norwegians.

After that, 10,000 Glaswegians.

Then Cambodians.

Then Estonians.

Somalis. Nepalis.

Syrians. Liberians.

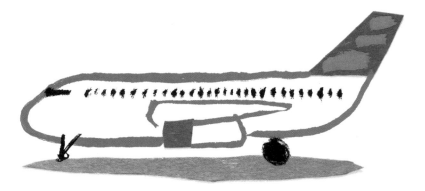

It never ends. It cannot end.

After all, the Statue of Liberty
is an immigrant, too.
And this is why she's moving.
This is why she's striding.

In welcoming the poor, the tired, the struggling to breathe free.

She is not content to wait.

She must meet them in the sea.

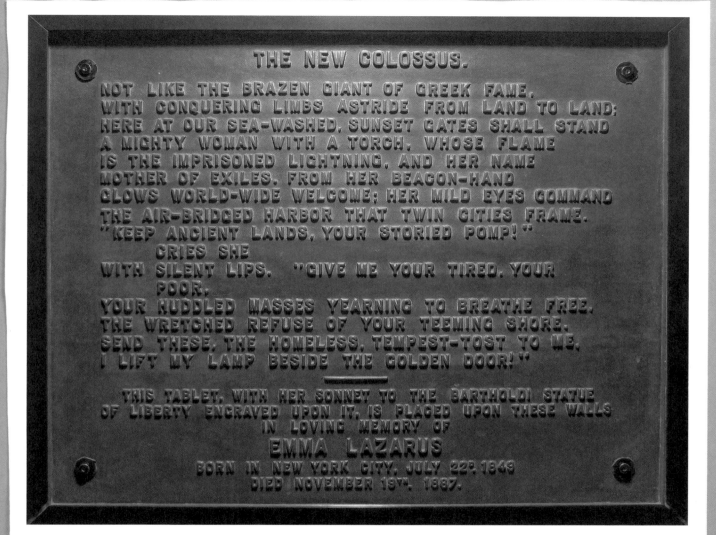

THE NEW COLOSSUS.

NOT LIKE THE BRAZEN GIANT OF GREEK FAME,
WITH CONQUERING LIMBS ASTRIDE FROM LAND TO LAND;
HERE AT OUR SEA-WASHED, SUNSET GATES SHALL STAND
A MIGHTY WOMAN WITH A TORCH, WHOSE FLAME
IS THE IMPRISONED LIGHTNING, AND HER NAME
MOTHER OF EXILES. FROM HER BEACON-HAND
GLOWS WORLD-WIDE WELCOME; HER MILD EYES COMMAND
THE AIR-BRIDGED HARBOR THAT TWIN CITIES FRAME.
"KEEP ANCIENT LANDS, YOUR STORIED POMP!"
      CRIES SHE
WITH SILENT LIPS. "GIVE ME YOUR TIRED, YOUR
      POOR,
YOUR HUDDLED MASSES YEARNING TO BREATHE FREE,
THE WRETCHED REFUSE OF YOUR TEEMING SHORE.
SEND THESE, THE HOMELESS, TEMPEST-TOST TO ME,
I LIFT MY LAMP BESIDE THE GOLDEN DOOR!"

THIS TABLET, WITH HER SONNET TO THE BARTHOLDI STATUE
OF LIBERTY ENGRAVED UPON IT, IS PLACED UPON THESE WALLS
IN LOVING MEMORY OF
EMMA LAZARUS
BORN IN NEW YORK CITY, JULY 22ᴰ 1849
DIED NOVEMBER 19ᵀᴴ, 1887.

Emma Lazarus wrote this poem to raise money for the construction of the pedestal the Statue of Liberty stands on. Now, the poem is engraved and posted at the Statue of Liberty National Monument.

FURTHER READING

Beaty, Andrea. *Iggy Peck, Architect.* New York: Harry N. Abrams, 2007.

Demuth, Patricia Brennan. *What Was Ellis Island?* New York: Grosset & Dunlap, 2014.

Glaser, Linda. *Emma's Poem: The Voice of the Statue of Liberty.* Boston: Houghton Mifflin Company, 2013.

Hearst, Michael. *Curious Constructions: A Peculiar Portfolio of Fifty Fascinating Structures.* San Francisco: Chronicle Books, 2017.

Holub, Joan. *What Is the Statue of Liberty?* New York: Grosset & Dunlap, 2014.

Hughes, Langston. *I, Too, Am America.* New York: Simon & Schuster, 2012.

Macaulay, David. *Building Big.* Boston: Houghton Mifflin Company, 2004.

Maestro, Betsy and Giulio. *The Story of the Statue of Liberty.* New York: HarperCollins Publishers, 1989.

Miller, Tom. *Seeking New York: The Stories Behind the Historic Architecture of Manhattan—One Building at a Time.* London: Pimpernel, 2015.

Moreno, Barry. *The Statue of Liberty Encyclopedia.* New York: Simon & Schuster, 2000.

Osborne, Linda Barret. *This Land Is Our Land: A History of American Immigration.* New York: Harry N. Abrams, 2016.

Peacock, Louise. *At Ellis Island: A History in Many Voices.* New York: Simon & Schuster, 2007.

Penner, Lucille Recht. *The Statue of Liberty (Step-into-Reading).* New York: Random House, 1995.

Rappaport, Doreen. *Lady Liberty: A Biography.* Somerville: Candlewick, 2011.

Ringgold, Faith. *We Came to America.* New York: Random House, 2016.

Sanna, Francesca. *The Journey.* London: Flying Eye Books, 2016.

Sasek, Miroslav. *This Is New York.* New York: Universe, 2003.

Say, Allen. *Grandfather's Journey.* New York: Houghton Mifflin Company, 2008.

Yolen, Jane. *Naming Liberty.* New York: Philomel Books, 2008.

SOURCES

Bell, James B., and Richard I. Abrams. *In Search of Liberty: The Story of the Statue of Liberty and Ellis Island.* New York: Doubleday, 1984.

Burns, Ric, and James Sanders. *New York: An Illustrated History.* New York: Alfred A. Knopf, 1999.

Hayden, Richard Seth, et al. *Restoring the Statue of Liberty: Sculpture, Structure, Symbol.* New York: McGraw-Hill, 1986.

Kaplan, Peter B., and Lee Iacocca. *Liberty for All.* Wilmington: Miller Publishing, Inc., 2002.

Mitchell, Elizabeth. *Liberty's Torch: The Great Adventure to Build the Statue of Liberty.* New York: Grove Press, 2014.

Rock, Howard, and Deborah Dash Moore. *Cityscapes.* New York: Columbia University Press, 2001.

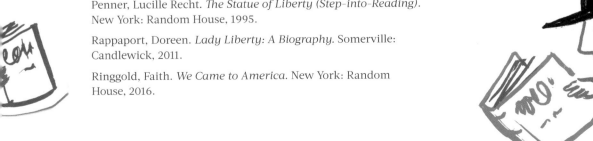